AS THOUGH I HAD WINGS

ung out too badly, staying clean for
much to the amazement of the fren
nded a monthly music specimen, but
et me off the hook. I began to get
usually upon the return of someone
Frankau in London. They would always
ece task of heroin and cocaine. Sometimes
ENE; Maurice Van Dero ex old lady
ch good; it had been stepped on so
t shoot a half a spoon to feel anything
in 20 mins. Madam Ricards "Chat
from all over Eur
d every night. Musicians, came in to
l of Madam Ricards home made chili. Up
out of the kitchen finally and a french
me his Flughorn, an old French Ilmar
it. He eventually gave it to me and
using it on all the albums I recor
"The best jazz album of 64-5", with
Charlie Rice - Junior Mance

chet baker

as though i had wings

the lost memoir

introduction by carol baker

a buzz book
st. martin's press new york

Design by Bryanna Millis

Library of Congress Cataloging-in-Publication Data

Baker, Chet.

As though I had wings : the lost memoir / Chet Baker.

p. cm.

ISBN 0-312-16797-0

1. Baker, Chet. 2. Jazz musicians—United States—Biography.

I. Title.

ML419.B14A3 1997

788.9'2165'092—dc21

[B] 97-14685

CIP

MN

First Buzz Books Edition: November 1997

10 9 8 7 6 5 4 3 2 1

Web site: http://buzzmag.com

acknowledgments

Carol Baker would like to thank the following:

The late Tom Baker for his friendship and his enormous help in the readying of this manuscript.

Steven Lowy for going above and beyond in the careful attention he gave to this project.

Jim Fitzgerald for recognizing the importance of this memoir and infecting others with his enthusiasm.

Dana Albarella for her unwavering love of Chet, his music, and his words.

introduction

All too often celebrities are reduced to one-dimensional caricatures. Public perception ends up defining the very boundaries of character, the circumference of the soul. This is too easy. There is always much more to a person than what the public gets to see, and never was this truer than in the case of Chet Baker. As Chet's wife, I know this more keenly than most.

Chet cannot be described as merely a musician, drug addict, husband, or legend. He was all of these and more, and this book is a testament to the fact. The decision to publish these memoirs was made with an eye toward the vibrancy and immediacy that Chet possessed—wonderful qualities that I didn't want to see lost via staid mentions within the dusty pages of jazz history, forgotten in the inadequacy of meager liner-note bios. Diluted reporting and secondhand retellings are not sufficient means to capture what Chet was—and maybe this book can't, either. But it comes close. These are his words, his memories, his perspectives. This is his story.

When Chet began to write about his life, it was not an attempt to exhaustively chronicle every day, every month, or even every year. Rather he sought to pull together a collection of memories that held special importance for *him.* Any competent biographer could piece together where Chet was and who he played with at any given time. But only Chet can tell you that Charlie Parker loved tacos with green sauce in between sets, or exactly what I was wearing the night he met my parents (green sequins—and in his words, I "looked beautiful").

As for my own memories of Chet, it would take another whole book to even scratch the surface: how sunlight played over his sharp cheekbones; the easy, loose curve of his arm as he held his trumpet; how his eyes deepened and went too far away when he played. Quick flashes of him that rise up unexpectedly and tighten my throat.

But, finally, all the reminiscences in the world only go so far. Chet's words go farther. In reading over this gorgeous jumble of images and impressions, I can only wonder at how accurately they reflect the very essence of Chet's life: unremitting chaos shot through with pure genius. Chet wouldn't have had it any other way.

carol baker, 1997

one

in the Rue de la Huchette called "La
che." An elderly woman named Madam Ricard owned the club
in an apartment upstairs. The apart
arranged in such a way that it
stitioned into 2 small apartments. A
s move upstairs. The police continue
me for a long time. Every month I'd rec
man from some inspector and within 24 hr
t myself to his office for an examination; if I
in in France. Business was good at the club
bring Dean down to the cave alley into to have he
down the bar; everyone wanted to hold him
with many European musicians during the next
Ottery and John Poole flew in from Denmark t
sh. The "Chez Ali" was in the algerian qua
from the Bastille. Two or three days a wee
with friends to sit drinking algerian tea
y one of the staff roll a huge cone shaped
. We would smoke and drink tea until
four when all the musicians came in. The
ttes, hand drums of all kinds, guitares, man
couple of guys could really sing. Stan
Allan Eager came through and as usual

Fort Lewis, Washington, seemed especially gray and cold during the winter of 1946–47, at least to me. I guess I had gotten used to the Southern California climate, where just a short time ago I'd spent so much time lying on the beach or skin-diving along the cliffs of Palos Verdes. About 85 percent of the guys in my barracks were from places like Georgia, Mississippi, and North and South Carolina. The men didn't seem overjoyed with where they were, but I can't remember any hassles between my fellow trainees during the long weeks of so-called ground-force training. We had the usual formations: marches, overnight bivouacs, hand grenade and M-1 qualifying, KP and guard duty; the same GI parties with big squares of lye soap and rough scrubbing brushes—unfortunate events that so many had been through before.

About a week before my company finished basic, I was called in to see the company commander. He explained that the Army knew I was only sixteen and that if at this moment I told him that I didn't want to remain in the Army, I would be discharged. I declined his offer and returned to my unit. I became friendly with a guy I met during training named Dick. He was from Pasadena, nineteen years old and really sharp, with an IQ of 148. He was strong, too, and could pull himself into a handstand on the parallel bar, swing all the way around, stop and then begin again, reversing his direction each time. He even knocked a guy unconscious one day coming out of the mess hall. As this guy, who was thirty-five to forty pounds heavier than Dick, was walking out, Dick moved his shoulders over to allow him to get by. This jerk then deliberately moved *his* shoulder over still further, and banged Dick's upper arm. Spinning around, Dick decked him, laying him flat out. As I said, he was a tremendously strong guy.

Dick and I were the only two out of our regiment to receive orders to ship to the Western theater of operations; everyone else went to Japan or Korea. After basic we were given a thirty-day leave, at the end of which we were shipped off to the East Coast (Camp Kilmer, New Jersey), then packed aboard a troopship, along with about 1,800 other guys, and sent on our way. The next ten days were like one long nightmare. The trip included the usual forty-eight-hour crap game, which I did not participate in, since the majority of the money always seemed to end up in the pockets of two or three guys. There was vomit everywhere, and you could not escape the smell of it no matter where you went on the ship. Since there wasn't anything alcoholic to drink, some of the guys mixed Aqua Velva with fruit juice. Everyone was getting loaded and fighting. Some went blind from the noxious aftershave mixture. Altogether, it was a trip I could not easily forget.

We finally landed at Bremerhaven and disembarked. Obviously, Dick and I were both happy to see the last of the good ship *General* ———. We spent our first night in Germany in a huge plane hangar discussing the events of our journey, likening it to a kind of fantastic rebirth process. We had left the womb ship where we had lived like packed maggots and now, with some rest, food, and fresh air, we were expected to change back into polished-booted, shiny-brassed defenders of our country.

The next morning, the men were fighting to get to the bulletin board, where they would find out what the Army intended to do with them, how long they'd have to do it, and where they would be stationed. Dick and I expected to finally be separated here at Bremerhaven, but the Army was sending us both to Berlin. Our train was stopped three times by the Russians and checked out thoroughly at each stop, and was finally allowed to pass through the rubble of bombed-out cities and snow-covered German countryside until we finally reached the Russian checkpoint on the outskirts of Berlin. We were once again checked, counted, and mostly just stared at by a company of riflemen just outside the train. The vibes these men gave off were strange and unfriendly; I wondered why. The destruction of Berlin was almost complete at this time, with buildings razed right down to the ground for blocks at a time. Russian tank divisions had roamed the streets of the city, taking revenge for what the Germans had done in Russia. They had left some blocks intact, though, and used these to house their own troops. These surviving apartment complexes—most of them about three stories high—were near the Office of Military Government in the American sector, where I was to work as a clerk typist and Dick was to take his assignment as a theater manager.

After billet assignment and the stowing of my gear, I was free to walk around the compound; naturally, I walked toward the sound of band music coming from somewhere nearby. I came to a door, the sign above it reading 298TH ARMY BAND. I walked into an orderly room where a master sergeant with an unsmiling, leathery face—he was about forty-five or fifty years old—sat at a desk in the corner with a four-foot brass-ended red, white, and blue–tasseled baton propped up behind him. He looked up and I started talking. I didn't stop speaking until I heard "Come around in the morning and you can talk to our first trumpet player." I left, thanking him profusely and eager to return.

The first trumpet player turned out to be a very nice guy named Martin who, after hearing me play a few minutes, said, "That's enough, Chet. I'll have the sarge make out a transfer request." They must have been hard up for trumpet players.

I spent the next year falling out—sometimes two to three times a week—in honor-guard uniform, being loaded into a truck and driven off to Tempelhoff Airport to pile out and wait for some congressman, senator, or four-star general to exit his plane. It wasn't so bad in the spring, summer, or fall, but the long German winter was a bitch, and it was rough standing out on the runway for up to three hours, often in four or five inches of snow, just to honor the arrival of these guys, most of whom really could not have cared less about the music that awaited them. They would inspect the band and the honor guard, with their chromed helmets and polished rifles flashing through the standard manual of arms—with some variations, of course. I remember thinking at the time, I wonder why those guys are all black and there are no black dudes in the band?

It was so cold in the winter you had to keep your mouthpiece in your mouth the whole time you stood there or else when you finally did touch your lips to the mouthpiece, it would freeze your lips to the metal. Sometimes the valves would freeze, too, so when it was time to play Martin, the bandleader, would tell the commanding officer, Hawk, "No music this time." Hawk never complained when this happened. He'd just nod his head, understanding that we had gone through all of this bullshit for nothing.

When spring came, the band began to have more time off, including several afternoons during the week, and Saturday and Sunday. I did a lot of bowling, played cards and Ping-Pong, and went to see Dick at his post in the big theater. It wasn't a public theater; only servicemen, officers, and their dependents could attend. It was one of the biggest movie houses I'd ever seen, even bigger than the Palladium in New York City. Dick had a staff of Germans working for him, his own office, a private room in the basement fixed up with a parachute that draped from the ceiling, colored lights, a bar, and his own 16mm projector—need I say more? Dick was a hell of a smart guy at nineteen. The Army wanted to send him to officers training school, but he didn't want any part of it. He had enlisted to keep from being drafted. If you enlisted, you pulled down your eighteen months and you were finished, but if you were drafted, you had to serve two years, and had no choice regarding your assignment. Dick did well. He was doing a tremendous black-market business, selling cameras, soap, chocolate, cigarettes, and the like. These items were what people used for money on the base, and if you had coffee, forget about it. It was one of the most valuable forms of currency going. Any soldier could flag down a VW with a German driver (as long as the driver was alone) and he'd take you anywhere for five to six cigarettes.

two

ransferred to another prison to await tri
days of "Pentonville" I went to court. I a
t take the whole thing too seriously. All i
gly pompous fools with their white wigs.
r, I was found guilty by his Lordship
believe the pharmacist's testimony that
n't ask him to steal the drugs and I ha
him anything for it. His Lordship sa
n't believe that I hadn't paid him to
tify. Back in "Pentonville" once again f
ys then to another prison where all the a
held and four days later I was accompan
ny and deported to France. Carol ~~was~~ and Dean, were
ry; She had arranged it with the po
~~[illegible]~~ We'd been back in
up when we were all picked up by the police
part of a 3 month investigation which
he arrest of about 150 people. We were a
n suspected drug addiction. After about 5
began to cop out. As soon as somebo
their statement admitting guilt, they
into another room and given a fix
rs better than they could get on the street,

As the weather got warmer that spring, I started spending more and more time at Lake Wansee, a spot on the edge of Berlin, bordering the Russian zone. It was a beautiful place. I started renting the sailboats, usually reserved for officers, and would sail for hours around the lake, with a portable radio blaring out Stan Kenton and Dizzy Gillespie. It was the first modern music I'd heard, and I couldn't believe it. This was the year that Stan Kenton came out with "Intermission Riff," "Artistry in Percussion," etc. And since we had a dance band made up of musicians from the Army Band that played almost every weekend at the NOO club, we were all interested in what was happening on the music scene.

I was pretty much a loner during that summer on the lake, and like most young guys, I had a fantasy about a woman. A woman that I dreamed I would meet somewhere on the lake, perhaps wading in the shallows along the shore, holding her dress up out of the water to keep it dry. She would be older than me, maybe twenty-two—blond, slender, and beautiful. I daydreamed of her often and never gave up on our eventual meeting. I knew it would happen.

At that time, I didn't smoke, so I saved all my cigarette rations to trade for different things. I had fourteen cameras, all different kinds. For ten cartons I had an oil painting made of my mom and dad from a color photo. I eventually got a beautiful gold ring with a two-carat aquamarine and two sapphires, which I later traded for a little one-cylinder motorboat that I used to get from shore out to the sailboat, which was tied to a buoy fifty yards offshore. She was thirty-eight feet overall with a steel hull and a rigged sloop that could sleep four. One day in midsummer I made my usual trip to the lake and, not caring about the poor weather, I jumped in my putt-putt and headed along the shore. All of a sudden, there she was, the very girl I'd pictured in my mind so many times. I headed toward her.

She was wading in a foot and a half of water, holding her cotton dress with one hand. She smiled as I pulled up beside her, and when I asked if she would like to go for a ride, she said, "I'd love to" in perfect English. She sat on the edge of the boat, lifted her legs and swiveled right on in next to me. She was really cute, even perfect you might say. For four months, I hadn't thought much about chicks. I'd say to myself, Why should I go out of my way to look for women when I'm sure that if I wait, it will be so much better?

As soon as she was next to me in the boat, it began to sprinkle, so I turned and headed for the sloop anchored two hundred yards away. We made it just in time, scampering into the dim cabin just as the big drops began to fall. The pounding of the rain on the deck helped to hide my own pounding heart. I had had a couple of experiences with girls, but they were just girls, if you know what I mean. Anyway, her name was Cisella, she was twenty-two, and for the next two hours I did my best to live up to the traditional American serviceman's standards.

I found out later that she and her sister were both being sent out by their mother and father in the hopes that they would meet a soldier—preferably an officer. The plan was for them to get married if possible—but not necessarily—and at the very least be taken care of with food from the PX, clothing, and money. Eventually, they hoped, this officer would arrange for the whole family to be shipped back to America and out of the living hell that it was for most Germans, especially in Berlin. They were both attractive girls. I heard later that Cisella's parents' plan worked, and she married a Russian officer. I'll never forget her and how she made my fantasy come true.

three

[illegible]
ransferred to another prison to await tri
days of "Pentonville" I went to court. I a
t take the whole thing too seriously. All i
gly pompous fools with their white wigs.
r, I was found guilty by his lordship
believe the pharmacist's testimony that
n't ask him to steal the drugs and I ha
him anything for it. His Lordship se
n't believe that I hadn't paid him to
tuff. Back in "Pentonville" once again f
ys then to another prison where all the a
held and four days later I was accompanie
ry and deported to France. Carol ~~was~~ and Sean were
ry; she had arranged it with the po
~~[illegible]~~ We'd been back in Pa
up when we were all picked up by the police
part of a 3 month investigation which
e arrest of about 150 people. We were a
n suspected drug addiction. After about 5
began to cop out. As soon as somebod
their statement admitting guilt, they
into another room and given a fix o
s better than they could get on the street.

At the end of October, I had an attack of appendicitis and spent sixty days in the hospital. Afterward, I was sent back to Camp Kilmer for discharge. I was ready. It was great to come home.

Hermosa Beach is usually sunny, with just enough ocean breeze to keep it from ever getting really hot. We lived on 16th Street, up the hill above the Pacific Coast Highway, for nearly four years. My mother had been working for W. T. Grant since I was about five years old; first in Oklahoma City, then in downtown L.A., and now, at this time, in Inglewood. My mother was a sweet and gentle woman, a country girl who'd been born in Yale, Oklahoma, just as I had. My father had met my mother while playing at Saturday-night barn dances. He played guitar very well, and he loved music. They were married soon after their meeting, and on December 23, 1929, I was born.

I remember everything about the farm where I was raised so well. There was a large red barn that, just looking at it from outside, you'd swear a strong breeze would carry the whole thing off, but when you went inside, aside from a few rotting boards here and there, the four-by-fours were in pretty good shape, and the entire structure was stable. It was a cool, shady place to hang out on hot afternoons.

There were cows, pigs, horses, chickens, ducks, cats, and dogs—and usually at least two or three nephews or nieces to play with as well. There was a hayloft to play hide-and-seek in, and I vividly remember all the childhood smells that the barn had. When I got a little older, I would accompany my dad and an uncle or two—my mother had four sisters and three brothers—through the blackjack trees in search of rabbits or a squirrel, and possibly a quail or two.

My grandfather was there when the Oklahoma Territory was opened up to the settlers. He had made that famous dash on horseback, along with thousands of others, and had managed to stake out an eighty-acre section for himself and for my grandmother. They had immigrated to the U.S., and they kept moving west, finally coming to rest in Oklahoma. He worked hard, as so many did, trying to eke out some kind of decent life for the two of them. By age twenty-nine, he had twenty acres of watermelon, peas, potatoes, corn, and all kinds of fruit trees, the most interesting of which was a lone persimmon tree that stood in the center of a large plowed field. To this very day I've never tasted any persimmon anywhere that came close to the flavor of the fruit that tree produced.

By the time the Depression came, my dad was a young

man and, of course, out of work. No one could afford to go dancing anymore, since just trying to survive was hard enough. He got one job, I remember, knocking down old steel boilers with a sixteen-pound sledgehammer; he made twenty-five cents an hour. Things finally got so bad that when I was one year old, we had to move from Yale to Oklahoma City, where my dad's sister, Agnes, lived. We stayed with my uncle Jim and aunt Agnes for six or seven years while I attended the Culbertson grammar school. My dad finally got work with the WPA as a timekeeper, and my mother found work in an ice-cream factory. She brought some home every night, and what a treat it was! Every flavor imaginable—a different one each night.

Every summer I'd spend a couple of months on the farm in Yale walking the dirt road that led to the highway, picking wild raspberries along the way. Often I'd walk out into the watermelons, pick one up over my head, and let it fall so that it split wide open. Then I'd eat the sweet heart out of it and leave the rest to the birds.

It was Aunt Agnes who took care of me from the time I was one until I was eight years old. She and Uncle Jim were the two most gentle people I think I've ever met. In all the time I spent with them, I don't ever remember either of them getting angry or raising their voice. "Darn" and "shucks" was about their limit when it came to cursing. Uncle Jim had fought somewhere in Flanders and had had his lungs burned badly by mustard gas. He worked for the city parks department, out in the fresh air cutting grass, trimming plants, and watering flowers. He loved to work outside, where he could breathe freely.

In all the time I lived with them, I never missed a day at school; I loved it, and got pretty good grades in every subject. But in 1940 we left Oklahoma and moved out to Glendale, California. 218 Everett Street. The schools in California were so much easier that they let me skip a half grade. I went to Glendale Junior High School, and then completed one year of high school before we moved again.

This time we wound up in North Redondo Beach, where we stayed with the Coulter family, some good friends of my folks who were also from Oklahoma. They had a son my age, Brad, a sweet, easygoing kid. We had a ball. He and I spent a lot of time messing with old cars. He built a little model of a Spider with a shortened drive shaft that went like hell—when it ran.

I became disenchanted with school during my junior year at Redondo High. I cut lots of classes and spent nearly every day on the beach or along the cliffs of Palos Verdes diving for abalone. My truancy didn't sit too well with my folks; we had a few family discussions about it, and finally I decided to join the Army.

four

gives birth. The government gives
for every new-born child, for blankets
and other stuff a baby needs. They
free milk for the first 6 mos. to
the child gets off to a good start. I
crazy around London and finally
into trouble with the law. Lady
write a script for friday, one for
for sunday because she always
country estate somewhere outside
weekends. As I cashed my
I noticed that there was a new
He seemed very friendly and
Since I hadn't much money
During lunch he said he like
wanted to help me out. I told him
need any help, that I got all the
on prescription. As I left I
appreciated his kindness but no thanks
at midnight, when the predated scripts
something. The addicts were lined up
their scripts filled and people were
up and down the line trying to get

By this time I had been playing around with the trumpet for about three years. My dad had brought home a trombone one day when I was thirteen years old. I'd been playing it for a couple of weeks without much success. Being small for my age, I just couldn't reach the bottom positions very well, and the mouthpiece was too big for my lips. After a couple of weeks, the trombone disappeared and was replaced by a trumpet. It was much more my size, and I was able to get a sound (of sorts) right away. I began to take an instrument course at school, but I had a lot of difficulty learning to read music. My problem was that I depended entirely on my ear, which caused no end of problems with the bandleader, Mr. Kay. I played in the marching band, where I learned all the Sousa marches by ear, and also played in the school dance band. My dad initially wanted me to play trombone because he was a great admirer of Jack Teagarden, but his disappointment diminished little by little as he watched my progress on the trumpet—see, he liked Bix, too.

By the time I returned to California after my Army discharge, my folks had been able to buy a clean little two-bedroom home at 1011 16th Street, in Hermosa Beach, up on the hill above Highway 101. This was the first home they had ever been able to own. In '49 I decided to take advantage of being eligible for GI benefits, so I enrolled in El Camino Junior College in Lawndale. My major would be music and my minor English. At school, I kept running into the same old problem: my ear. El Camino, at that time, wasn't really like a real college; the classes were held in what looked suspiciously to me like old Army barracks.

It was while attending El Camino that I became acquainted with Andy Lambert; he had a brother, Jack, who was beginning his career as a movie-actor heavy. Andy played bass in a trio in Hermosa Beach at a joint called the High Seas. He was in his thirties and had been in the Navy, where he had lost a leg. He now got around nicely on a wooden peg. We became friends, and he invited me to come into the club and sit in with his band.

Andy was also the first person to turn me onto grass, bless him; I loved it, and continued to smoke grass for the next eight years, until I began chipping and finally got strung out on stuff. I enjoyed heroin very much, and used it almost continually, in one form or another, for the next twenty years (if you include methadone, which does not provide a feeling of euphoria at all, unless you're clean).

So I did sit in at the Seas, and got good vibes from Andy and the guitarist, Gene Sergeant, but the leader of the band, the piano player (who played well), seemed to resent me. Actually, he appeared to be the type who would resent anyone who might push into his spotlight. Gene and Andy liked my playing, though, and through them I met Jimmy Rowles, who at that time was pianist for Peggy Lee at Ciro's on Sunset Boulevard. Gene paid my union dues, lying and saying that the group was supposed to go to Bombay, of all places, and that he needed me to go along. Kane, the jealous piano player, nixed the deal; I figured he would.

After that, as often as I could, I would show up at Jimmy Rowles's pad between noon and one o'clock—sometimes he'd even be asleep when I arrived—but he was always great to me, and would always invite me in. I'd wait for him to eat breakfast and then I'd ask him to play some tunes for me. It seemed like he knew more damn songs than anybody had ever known. All the good ones, anyway. I learned a lot about keeping things simple, and about not getting too busy on my horn, from him.

It seems to me that most people are impressed with just three things: how fast you can play, how high you can play, and how loud you can play. I find this a little exasperating, but I'm a lot more experienced now, and understand that probably less than 2 percent of the public can really hear. When I say *hear,* I mean follow a horn player through his ideas, and be able to understand those ideas in relation to the changes, if the changes are completely modern. Dixie is different—it's easier to follow, and rock is even simpler than Dixie, except for the music of a few really fine rock musicians (or variations thereof) like Herbie Hancock, John Scofield, Mike and Randy Brecker, and a few others.

During this period I made it to many sessions around L.A., as there was somewhere to play almost every night. Each Sunday, there was a session from 2:00 P.M. till 2:00 A.M. that Howard Rumsey—don't ask me how—was the leader of, and because of this fact, the only time it would swing was when another bass player sat in. Howard Rumsey was the only bass player I knew of (professional) who played right in the middle of the beat. If you tried to do it on purpose, it would be very difficult, but for Howard it was apparently no problem. In spite of this drawback, I learned a lot from the good musicians who would occasionally come and sit in. People like Shelly Manne, Shorty Rogers, Hampton Hawes, Dexter Gordon, Sonny Clark, Frank Morgan, Stan Levey, Lawrence Marable, Bill Holman, Art Pepper, Bob Whitlock, Monty Budwig, and many others.

At this time, however, the best sessions were out in the Valley. I'm sure some Californians remember the "Showtime" out on Sepulveda Boulevard. Well, the first few times I went out there, I was not allowed to play, but then finally I was allowed to sit in one time, on just one set—you see, it was rather cliquey. Herbie Harper ran the gig, and the rhythm section was usually Joe Mondragon, Shelly, and maybe Lou Levy or Jimmy Rowles. After a while, I finally got to play a whole set; then two sets, and eventually it became my gig and everyone had to ask me if they could get in. Dave Pell was around then, and so was Steve White. Joe Maine, Herb Geller, Frank Rosalino, a trumpet player named Kenny Bright who just seemed to disappear, and Conte Candoli and Jack Sheldon. There were so many wonderful guys, Al Porcino and Claude and Stu Williamson, Dexter Gordon, Lonnie Miehause, Jack Montrose, Bob Gordon, Red Mitchell, Harry Babason, Oscar Pettiford, Lawrence Marable, Sonny Criss, Frank Morgan, and Russ Freeman. I even went up to Santa Barbara a couple of times to a session and met Bill Perkins there.

Sometimes I'd go down to Manhattan Beach to a place called Esther's, where the great Matt Dennis worked. He was a hell of a nice guy, and I'd always ask him to do his tune "Everything Happens to Me." He'd let me sit in sometimes. They eventually started having regular sessions there, and after a few weeks I met the second (Cisella being the first) of what has turned out to be a long list of very lovely ladies.

five

friend in his life. I gave him a fit. ...
... quit her job in ITALY and began travelin
with me, all kinds of stories about me and ab
hed her father and mother. One story was s
I had abducted Carol, and was keeping her a
inst her will by giving her heroin. That story
came out in a scandal paper in London. Natu
rols father started getting phone calls about
ding all the bullokis in the papers, he decided
t for himself. He and Carols mother arrived
e evening while I was appearing at an exclu
lub on the via Veneto, the Rupe Tarpea. One lo
Carol and they knew everything was cool, she was
n a dark green sequined evening dress and s
utiful. He explained about all the publicity
he papers. One newspaper even print a story
looking for us. They remained in Roma a coup
d returned to England, satisfied that their dau
t being abused by some maniac, but they wa
now. I was using again and Carol was
. Under the circumstances, I'd have to give
. A for remaining cool and calm; most g
I found out later that most of the stories abo

Sherry was a tiny, shapely, very attractive eighteen-year-old, and it was love at first sight. We went everywhere together for the next few months, but then she got pregnant. I brought her home to stay with me and my folks, to try and figure out what the hell to do. My folks were great about it, and even helped me locate a doctor to remedy our situation. Sherry was such a sweet baby that I would have married her and let her have the child, but since I had practically no income and no place of my own to live, my parents began to pressure me to break it off with her. Perhaps they feared that she would get pregnant again, or maybe it was simply for economic reasons. Anyway, I sure missed having her around and remember her from time to time with warmth and affection. I hope that she found happiness and love with someone worthy of her.

Not long after all of this occurred, I decided to break away from home once again and moved in with three of the outest cats imaginable. Jimmy McKean was a drummer of unusual talent; completely ambidextrous and reputed to have one of the biggest wangs west of the Sierra Madres. Manuel was a completely spaced-out guy, a non-musician whose main object in life seemed to be to find out how much grass he could smoke up before the second coming of Christ. Finally, Don Sparky will be remembered by a few Inglwoodians for his antics in the drug scene, which eventually killed him. Jimmy is gone now, too, but in 1950 we were all very much alive, and we never had less than a kilo or two around. Sometimes we would all sit around a low coffee table with piles of clean grass in front of us and loose papers at the ready, seeing who could roll the most joints (commercial) in an hour. Don always took care of copping and he and Manuel were heavy into the two-joints-for-a-dollar market (or lids, or anything really). Whatever it was, Don knew where to get it wholesale. He was a brilliant guy.

We all got along pretty well that summer of '50. I had to quit El Camino in the middle of my second year. My music teacher told me I'd never make it as a musician, and as I had never desired to be an English teacher, I quit. I continued to play and make all the sessions I could. You could expect to see me almost anywhere in L.A. County where there was a session going on. This drummer Bob Neel and I became pretty tight and ran around together quite a bit, dropping in on Russ Freeman almost every day.

Hermosa Beach in the summer of '50 was jumping, with hundreds of beautiful young things lying all over the place and guys walking up and down the Strand, flexing their muscles and talking hip. They tried to attract the

females in somewhat the same manner as male peacocks might. But inside the Lighthouse on Sundays was the best, with the beautiful people coming in their swimsuits, sitting along the bar or at a table, sipping cool beers and digging the music. The only drawback was a big, dumb plainclothes cop, who would come in and stand around to see if there was anyone he could fuck with. His name was Charlie something and he was what most people would call a real asshole. He acted as if he had been commissioned by God to put a damper on everyone's fun. He never bothered me, but some of his fellow officers fucked with many a musician friend of mine when they left the club to drive home. I hated these bastards and all they stood for, and I think he knew this, but as long as I was clean, I had no problem. But I don't want to get into the police stories yet; that will come later.

One day I spotted this beautiful blonde sitting at the bar. I had seen her a couple of times before and had told myself that I would hit on her if she came in again. When the set broke, I worked my way through the packed club until I was beside her. I can't remember what I said exactly, but within half an hour we were parked in her father's new Buick along the cliffs of Palos Verdes. Her name was Charlaine, and she was really something. We made it a lot during the next two to three months—she

loved to be screwed and I loved screwing her. Once, in front of her house in Lynwood, we made it nine times in three hours. I really had it bad for Charlaine, but I wasn't alone. There was another dude who also liked her action. Charlaine and I eventually argued over this and some other stuff, and because of it I reenlisted directly into the Sixth Army Band up in San Francisco, a three-year commitment.

six

friend in his life. I gave him a fit.
quit her job in ITALY and began travel
with me, all kinds of stories about me and a
ched her father and mother. One story stated
I had abducted Carol, and was keeping her
inst her will by giving her heroin. That sto
came out in a scandal paper in London. Natu
rols father started getting phone calls about
ding all the bullshit in the papers, he decide
t for himself. He and Carols mother arrived
e evening while I was appearing at an exclu
club on the via Veneto, the Rupe Tarpea. One lo
Carol and they knew everything was cool, she wa
in a dark green sequined evening dress and
utiful. He explained about all the publicity
the papers. One newspaper even print a story
looking for us. They remained in Roma a coup
d returned to England, satisfied that their daug
t being abused by some maniac, but this wa
now. I was using again and Carol was
t. Under the circumstances, I'd have to give
th A for remaining cool and calm; most of th
I found out later that most of the stories ab

The Presidio was a beautiful post near Golden Gate Bridge, surrounded by a forest of dark pine trees. It didn't take me long to find out where everything was happening. I met and sat in with Cal Tjader at Facks, Dave Brubeck and Paul Desmond at the Blackhawk, and was a regular at Bop City, an after-hours club that didn't open until two in the morning. Wigmo was around, and Johnny Baker and Frank Foster (who was also in the Army) would come in and play. Pony Poindexter, too. After six months of my nightly wanderings around Frisco, Charlaine and I had a reconciliation, and we were married in Las Vegas while I was on a three-day pass, after which we moved into a room on Lombard Street. From then on, being in the Sixth Army Band was like a day gig. Each day I'd make it for reveille (roll call), make the morning band rehearsal, and usually be free in the afternoon to go home and crash. I'd then get up at midnight and go play at Bop City till around five-thirty, rush to the base, make roll call, etc., on and on. For months I did this, until I felt I'd had enough of the Army, and devised what I felt was a workable idea to get a discharge.

Right about this same time, two flute players had managed to get out. One guy put himself into a trance, and while I didn't see this myself, I was told of his being carried out of the band barracks by two medical corpsmen:

One held his feet while the other held his shoulders, using no stretcher. He was stiff as a board, and none of their attempts to bring him out of it worked, including the jabbing of a pin into the bottom of his feet. The other guy told the bandleader that there was a little man inside of his flute who was playing all the wrong notes. They both got out.

My plan wasn't that simple, but it was simple enough, really. Across the street that ran along the back of the barracks there was a dense growth of bushes, which I began using as my own private toilet. I did this for about a month and then made an appointment with the post psychiatrist, a young lieutenant who was very nice but somewhat inexperienced. He gave me all the required tests; showed me ink blots, and had me fill out a 650-multiple-answer questionnaire that the Army felt would tell them exactly where my head was at. There were questions like "If you had your choice, would you rather be a forest ranger, a mechanic, or a florist?" I'd always pick the most feminine answer. I told him I'd been smoking grass for years; I told him I couldn't use the toilet in the barracks in the morning with all the other guys, for even though I lived off the post, I had to be in the barracks all day. I explained how I felt uncomfortable to the point of not being able to sit in that row of toilets and do something that I felt should be done in private, etc., etc. I said lots of crazy things. After I finished the tests and the questions, the doctor explained that it would take some time to get the results of the tests, and that it might even take as long as two weeks before he could tell me what the outcome would be.

A week later I got transferred to Fort Huachuca, Arizona. It seems that an order came down from some brass somewhere that a band was to be formed of all bandsmen who could not pass a sight-reading test or who were fuck-ups in some way, like being suspected of smoking grass or playing crazy. There I was, plucked out of my comfortable S.F. routine and separated from my wife, plopped down out in the middle of nowhere. I hung on for about sixty days, but finally I couldn't stand it anymore and I went AWOL. I found out later that after I went AWOL, about a third of the band followed suit, and that the warrant officer in charge of the band had a nervous breakdown and had to take a long rest. Every once in a while I run into someone who was there at that time, and we reminisce about those days and how high everybody was—the Mexican border was only thirty miles from Fort Huachuca, and grass was only thirty dollars a kilo.

seven

thing out too badly, staying clean for
much to the amazement of the fre
ended a monthly urine specimen, but
let me off the book. I began to get
usually upon the return of someone to
Frankau in London. They would alway
rees taste of heroin and cocaine. Sometim
RENE; Maurice Van Ness ex old lady w
uch good; it had been stepped on so
to shoot a half a spoon to feel anything
in 20 mins. Madam Ricards. Chat ch
ed every night. Musicians, from all over E, came in to
owl of Madam Ricards home made chile. Up
out of the kitchen finally and a fren
t me his Flugelhorn, an old French
of it. He eventually gave it to me and
s, using it on all the albums I reco
ix." The best jazz album of 64-5, with
Charlie Rice, Jimi Hendrix, Bobby T

Returning to L.A., I enjoyed a wonderful month with my young and beautiful wife. Charlaine was living in a small bungalow behind her father's Lynwood home. We spent a loving, leisurely month together. Each night I'd pick Charlaine up at the dress shop where she'd found work and we'd go somewhere. Things were good between us during this time. I had explained everything to her about what I'd done in Presidio with respect to my attempt to get out of the Army, and she knew that what I had to do was not going to be pleasant, but that it was the only way.

Returning to San Francisco, I turned myself into the young lieutenant shrink who had examined and tested me before. He seemed like a nice guy. He explained how, had I not been transferred, I would have been given a discharge on the basis of my test results and his investigation. He could not explain why, though, that if my case warranted immediate discharge while I was stationed at the Presidio, it didn't warrant my immediate discharge while I was at Fort Huachuca. The lieutenant accompanied me to the office of the MPs, and I soon found myself in the stockade, a situation that I had to remedy as quickly as possible. I spent a couple of days with the rest of those poor bastards, walking all over the post, picking up anything and everything that didn't belong there. We were guarded by MPs with shotguns and returned each evening to fall in, march around, and do a lot of push-ups. It was during this time each night that someone would manage to shove a towel into a truck gas tank so that later on those who wanted to could get high sniffing it. I don't know how they managed to get that stinking towel in the lockup every night, since we were all searched. Later, watching a few guys sniff that towel, I flashed back to when I had gone out as a kid, during the war, and siphoned gas out of some guy's car, and how stoned I got, a few of these times. If someone had come out and caught me, I wouldn't have been able to move. Reliving those moments, my eyes fixed on nothing, I was snapped back by a tap on the shoulder; some guy offering me the towel. He shrugged and turned away when I said, "No thanks, I feel shitty enough." Well, I did. I then lapsed back into my daydreaming, my mind running over the events of my past. I got caught up completely, and the next thing I knew I was being lifted and supported by two guards and helped down to a private cell on the ground floor. Someone handed me a red and said, "Take that and get some rest." I was awakened the next day by the sound of keys and gates banging open and shut, the guards yelling their orders to the prisoners to line up and fall out; then it was quiet and I realized that I was being kept in. A half hour later, I was told that I was being sent to the closed station off the neuropsychiatric ward.

I was put into a cell with a guy who was supposedly suffering from shell shock. He was as cool and easygoing as you like during the day—it was night that he came alive. Four or five times during the next three weeks I was awakened by this guy's yelling as he stood on his bed, eyes closed, kicking and swinging at some imaginary enemy. Then the gate would slide open and in would rush three or four attendants. I don't know how he was able to connect with his eyes closed, but those guys really had to work to get a straitjacket on him and strap him back in bed. Some of these patients were on thyroxine, Elavil, Stellazine, phenobarbital. Some of them were getting shock treatment. You'd see a couple of attendants escort some guy out, and five minutes later you'd hear him yell a couple of times—really terrifying yells—and then they'd carry him back to his cell, hanging, unconscious, between them.

I had a daily visit by one "Captain K," who was in charge of the ward. He'd ask me questions, write things down on his little pad, and within five minutes move to the next patient. You can imagine how I felt when they told me at the end of three weeks that I was to be granted a discharge. It was a general discharge, which meant that I was deemed "unadaptable to Army life." I was immediately transferred to the regular outpatient open ward to await discharge.

eight

in the Rue De La Hachette called "La
eche." An elderly woman named Madam Ricard owned the club
in an apartment upstairs. The apar
arranged in such a way that it
artitioned into 2 small apartments, a
to move upstairs. The police continu
me for a long time. Every month I'd rec
gram from some inspector and within 24 h
ent myself to his office for an examination; if I
ain in France. Business was good at the club
bring Dean down to the cave alley, into her be
l down the bar; everyone wanted to hold her
with many European musicians during the next
O'Day and John Poole flew in from Denmark
ash. The "Chez Ali" was in the Algerian qu
from the Bastille. Two or three days a wee
with friends to sit drinking Algerian tea
ing one of the staff roll a huge cone shape
t. We would smoke and drink tea until
four when all the musicians come in. T
utes, hand drums of all kinds, guitars, ma
couple of guys could really sing. Stan
llan Eager came through and as usual

Again in L.A., I soon found work with Vido Musso, who, after having been with Stan Kenton for a while and having recorded "Come Back to Sorrento," was able to get a band together and to work. My old friend Jimmy McKean was playing drums, Gil Barrios was on piano, and I can't remember who the bassist was; it may have been Monty Budwig. After playing for a while with Vido, I went with Stan Getz's band; that was a real experience. At this point, I had still never been strung out on stuff, but I had tried it a few times, and usually, since it was pretty good quality back then, ended up really loaded and puking my guts up. I promised myself over and over that I would never take it again.

One day, Jymie Merritt and I went to see Larry Bangham, and we could hear an old pump organ spewing out Bach as we walked up the driveway. The music came from a small shack in the backyard. We knocked and the music stopped, and a second later the door cracked open, revealing the soundproofed interior. We were invited in, and Jymie immediately lit up a joint and we discussed getting together to play sometime soon. A few weeks later Larry, Jimmy McLeller, Bob Whitlock, and I moved into what used to be the separate servants' quarter of a large mansion along the esplanade in Redondo Beach. Larry got ahold of a 3/4 piano somewhere, and balanced the action and tuned it. He played for hours every day. He had a way playing out of meter that seemed to hang everybody up when he played with other musicians, but by himself he was something else. Not that we didn't play a lot together, the four of us.

At this time, Bob was working for George Shearing, Jymie was playing some gigs with Freddie "Schnicklefritz" Fisher, and I was working with Stan Getz. Larry just played and played, but after a couple of years of being on the scene and having little success, he gave up playing and took up painting. He got a job at Pittsburgh Paints, mixing paint, and within a few months was painting seascapes from memory. He would drive up along the Palos Verdes cliffs, stop and stare down at the waves crashing against a line of reefs, and then come back and paint what he had seen. I often wonder what happened to Larry Bangham.

One day during the summer of '52 I returned home to find a telegram under the door. It was from Dick Bock, I believe, and it said that Charlie Parker was auditioning trumpet players for some club dates in California. The audition was to take place that same day at three o'clock at the Tiffany Club. I rushed over, arriving a little late, and I could hear Bird from outside as he ran through a tune with some trumpet player. Pushing into the darkened club, I could make out Bird up on the stand flying through the blues. I sat for a minute or two, looking around the room. I recognized many trumpet players and lots of other people I knew who somehow had found out about Bird being there. I saw someone move up to the band-stand and say something to Bird. I felt uncomfortable and very nervous as he asked the crowd if I was in the club, and would I come up and play something with him. He had bypassed all these other guys, some of whom had much more experience than I had and could read anything you put in front of them.

We played two tunes. The first was "The Song Is You," and then a blues song written by Bird called "Cheryl," in the key of G, which, luckily, I knew. After "Cheryl," he announced that the audition was over, thanked everyone for coming, and said that he was hiring me for the gig. We did two weeks at the Tiffany, playing with Scatman Crothers—actually, it may have been Harry the Hipster. At any rate, it was incredible being on the stand with Bird. The first tune every night was fast, after which the rest of the night was easy. Bird was a flawless player, and although he was snorting up spoons of stuff and drinking fifths of Hennessy, it all seemed to have little or no effect on him. I wondered at the stamina of the man. He treated me like a son, putting down any and all guys who tried to offer me some shit.

During the breaks I'd drive him over to a taco stand a few blocks away and he'd eat a dozen *tacitos* with green sauce; he loved 'em. Sometimes, in the afternoon, we would drive down to the beach or around the Palos Verdes–San Pedro coastline. Bird would get out along the cliffs and stare out to sea, or watch the waves breaking on the rocks below for half an hour. I'm sure he liked California very much, for he enjoyed the open spaces, the beach, and the chicks. We played a few gigs for Billy Berg, and the old 54 Ballroom on 54th and Central was packed for Bird. There were hundreds of smiling black people giving him the respect and admiration that he so richly deserved. He made them happy, he made them dance, and he entertained them with his ideas and his heart. They loved him.

We had just finished a short tour up in North Bakersfield, San Francisco, Seattle, and Vancouver along with Dave Brubeck and Ella Fitzgerald, and were into our third night at a club called the Say When when we got fired. It just so happened that during our engagement there was a big telethon benefit for muscular dystrophy that we appeared on, as did almost every entertainer who happened to be in the Bay Area at the time. It was quite an affair, with people phoning in their pledges of donations from restaurants, clubs, and hotels, as well as private residences. We finished our TV appearance and returned quickly to do our first set at the club. When we were through, Bird got on the microphone and announced that he was passing the hat among the customers, with the proceeds to go to the Muscular Dystrophy Association, and that the club had agreed to equal whatever was collected. He did this, of course, completely on his own, without having spoken to the manager of the club, who was a tough guy named Dutch. Anyway, after the money was collected, Bird walked over to the bar, with all the eyes and ears in the joint focused on his counting out the money. The total came to $125. Naturally, Dutch refused to kick in his $125. People began yelling, banging on the tables, etc.; there was almost a riot, and as I said, that was the end of our engagement. Later that morning Bird must have fallen asleep with a cigarette in his hand and set his mattress on fire. He was staying in a hotel across the street, and we were all awakened by the arrival of the fire department and the subsequent tossing of Bird's mattress out into the street. Oh Bird, never a dull moment.

Charlie Parker returned to New York and I went back to L.A., where I worked a few nights at Seal Beach with Freddie "Schnicklefritz" Fisher. After playing with Bird, it was like one extreme to the other. Freddie must have been sixty at the time. He was a Dixieland clarinet player who brightened up his act with an unusual bit: He had a big rubber mat of proudly shaped ladies' breasts that he would toss on the floor. Then, taking off his shoes and socks, he would prance around on the mat while uttering all kinds of absurd, dirty little things. I could hardly play most of the time from laughing so hard. He thought I played a lot like Bix, and it was fun playing a little Dixie, but it wasn't really what I had in mind. Like most guys interested in jazz, I had heard Miles's album *Birth of the Cool* when it came out in '48, with arrangements by Gerry Mulligan, compositions by Mulligan, John Carisi, and Gil Evans, and loaded with talented guys like Lee Konitz, J.J. Johnson, and Max Roach. Even today, nearly thirty years later, I still listen to it often.

When I heard that Gerry had hitchhiked to L.A. from New York, and that he was interested in putting together a group, I was curious to find out about this guy. A couple of weeks later I was called in for a rehearsal with Mulligan, which turned into a big hassle between Gerry and some chick who had come with him from New York. She played the maracas—somewhat—but mostly she was just a pain in the ass for Gerry and kept anything from happening with her bullshit. He got in touch with me a week later and we set up another meeting, this time at my house. Chico Hamilton, Bob Whitlock, Gerry, and myself were present. The group clicked immediately under Gerry's direction, and a couple of weeks later we began what turned out to be an eleven-month run at a little club across from the Ambassador Hotel called the Haig.

It was a tiny club seating only about eighty-five people. It had originally been a private house, but someone had torn out a wall or two and converted it into an intimate little room for music with a small bar, about twelve stools, and maybe fourteen or fifteen tables. The band was an instant success. We received a lot of publicity and were recorded by Dick Clark, in cooperation with Roy Halt, and Pacific Jazz Records was born. Bob Whitlock stayed on with the band for a couple of months but then decided he wanted to go to college and was replaced by Carson Smith.

It was around this time that I got busted for the first time. It happened one night during a break. I was sitting in my car in the parking lot getting high with two other musicians when a police car came through and, seeing us, stopped. I tossed the grass into the well of the car but they found it. The two other guys had been busted before, so we quickly arranged between the three of us that I would say it was mine, since first offenders were usually given probation. I got out on bail the next morning, but they took my car. The cops who busted me were complete dummies who loved to harass and bust musicians, actors, and celebrities of all kinds; people who were an easy bust, and who would get their names in the paper. They never arrested the pushers or anyone who might be really dangerous. It wasn't their style.

The band continued to draw very well, with people lined up outside on the weekends. Gerry got married to a waitress at the club named Jeffie, and Charlaine and I moved into a house with them in Hollywood. Gerry was not an easy person to get along with, especially since he was using. He was nervous and high-strung, and sometimes I'd notice how much his long fingers would tremble as he played his horn. At this point, I'd been to court, gotten my three years' probation, and had been back to work about a month or so when one night, around midnight, in run two cops, pulling everyone off the stand and really leaning on Gerry. They would only tell me that I was under arrest, but they took Gerry to one side, and what they said was really upsetting him. He must have been confused, because he ended up going back to the house and leading them right to where he had his stuff and his kit buried, along the side of the house.

Actually they had nothing on him, but they scared him into believing he was going to get some heavy time—or they were going to kick his ass—if he didn't cop out. They had parked an unmarked car at an angle into Jeffie's little

Hillman Minx, then they rang the doorbell. Jeffie could see a car angled into hers when she looked out through the curtain. She went to the door and heard a man say, "Is this your little white car in the front? I'm hung up on your bumper." Charlaine, who didn't believe it from shit, had taken the grass and locked herself into the back toilet, and was flushing it just as Jeffie cracked the door to give the man her car keys—as I said, she was young. They crashed through the door, nearly knocking Jeffie flat, and ran toward the sound of the flushing toilet. As they pounded on the door and threatened what they were going to do if she didn't open up, Charlaine snapped the lock open and stepped calmly out. There was just enough grass still floating around in the toilet so that if they wanted to get it out, they could legally file on someone. Well, these two gallant officers did get it out. They performed an illegal act to gain access with no warrant, collected not even enough evidence to weigh, and busted three people (Jeffie, Charlaine, and myself—and I wasn't even there). The state narcotics officer, a guy named O'Conner, had by this time heard about the methods of these two cops, who both worked for the city or the county. He was able to keep at least some kind of check on their activities. His being a state officer must have intimidated them, but if he wasn't on the scene, they could be treacherous.

The night they busted us, they took Gerry and me back to the house. I went inside and Gerry went with the cops down the driveway to the back corner of the house, and confusedly he gave them the evidence they needed. Before that moment, they could have only charged him with having marks. We were all booked, locked up for an hour, and then released on bail—except Gerry. We all pleaded not guilty, went to court, and beat it—except Gerry. It was like he was there one minute and gone the next; we didn't see each other for six months. He never contacted me or wrote me a letter from jail.

Even though Gerry had been using, he took care of business as far as music was concerned, and he put together a nice little band. It sounded so good some nights; a completely different sound without a piano. We made several albums during the Mulligan Quartet's stay at the Haig, several for Pacific Jazz and one or two for Fantasy. Now that I look back, it seems amazing that we managed to stay together as long as we did. Gerry won first place in *Down Beat* and *Metronome* as best baritone player and I won on trumpet while he was gone. I took over leadership of the band at this point, making Russ Freeman the musical director and hiring Bob Neel to play drums.

Chico left to form his own group, but Larry Bunker and Carson stayed on bass. We recorded a few albums for Pacific Jazz: quartet instrumentals, vocals with the quartet, vocals with Russ Freeman, Shelly Manne and strings. We performed as a sextet with Shelly, Russ, Brookmeyer, and Bud Shank, and as an octet, with all the guys I mentioned before and Jack Montrose and Bob Gordon. I recorded an album for Columbia (arranged by Shorty Rogers and Marty Paich) with Zoot, Bud Shank, Shelly, Russ, and Mondragon, with the strings produced by Dick Bock for George Avakian. Dick Bock is one of the nicest men I've met in this business since I began to play, over thirty-five years ago.

One afternoon, about six months later, I happened to be walking down Hollywood Boulevard and walked into Gerry and Arlene Brown. I didn't like her vibes instantly. It seems Gerry was divorcing Jeffie and planned to marry Arlene, which to my way of thinking had to be something like being in heaven one second and in hell the next. Arlene was a short Jewish woman—not attractive, and looking as though she would gain weight easily; of course, I didn't know about her mind. She must have given Gerry something he needed, but on a purely physical basis, Jeffie was sweet and beautiful while Arlene was just a drag. We spoke right there on the street for a few minutes, then I said that I'd work for Gerry again, and that I didn't care what we did—club dates, concerts, whatever—but I wanted three hundred dollars a week. "Not a lot of money under the circumstances," I said. They both started laughing, saying that it was too much. After saying good-bye and good luck to Gerry, I walked off. It was some time before I saw him again. He had married Arlene and they'd had a son, Reed. They were now divorced and he was with a singer named Georgia Brown.

After my conversation with Gerry that day, I signed a contract with Joe Glazer (ABC Booking) and along with Russ and Bob Carson I began to travel east. I bought a Jaguar, taking over the payments from a guy I knew in Inglewood who was strung out and going to lose it. I gave him three hundred dollars and took over his equity. It was just six months old, a dark-green standard roadster that would have caused me a lot of trouble with the police, if they had caught me.

I vividly remember driving down a long, smoothly paved stretch of Route 66, coming into Albuquerque. My tach was 6800, and I was doing around 135 mph. It was incredible. I loved that roadster, but it was so damn cold at 85 to 90 mph in the winter with that little cloth top and the side curtain. Your feet would be okay, but from the waist up, forget it. Russ wouldn't ride with me no matter what the temperature was; I took him on a ride through L.A. traffic once that ended in his pleading with me to stop and let him out. He never got in a car I was driving after that.

We left L.A. and headed toward New York in a new Mercury four-door, pulling a small trailer and my roadster. We played the old Blue Note in Chicago with Erroll Garner opposite us on the bill, the Rouge Lounge outside Detroit, the Blue Note in Philadelphia, and Storyville in Boston. We headed up to Toronto to the Colonial Inn, performed a few college concerts, and then went back to Frisco and the Blackhawk, where I had played with Brubeck a few years before.

Back in New York, I met a Parisian girl named Liliane. She was just twenty-two, and she traveled with me for the next two years. Charlaine and I had been drifting for some time, and Liliane was like a breath of fresh air. She was quick, beautiful, and played chess well. In L.A. we did more recording, and I worked in a movie with John Ireland. I didn't dig it too much; having to get up early in the morning, get to the studio, be made up, and then sit around inside the set while they set up the scene, the lighting, etc. I used to climb up to the top of the set when I got really bored. The picture, *Hell's Horizon,* was made in ten days. Bill Williams, Hugh Beaumont, Jerry Paris, and Marla English were some of the people involved in the film.

nine

... Rue de la Huchette, called La
...che." An elderly woman named Madam Ricard owned the club
...in an apartment upstairs. The apar...
arranged in such a way that it...
...rtitioned into 2 small apartments. ...
...s move upstairs. The police continue...
...me for a long time ~~months~~. Every month I'd see...
...name from some inspector and within 24 h...
...t myself to his office for an examination; if I...
...in in France. Business was good at the club...
...ring Sean down to the cave every nite ~~out~~ to he...
...down the bar; everyone wanted to hold him...
...with many European musicians during the next ...
...Olsey and John Poole flew in from Denmark to...
...sh. The "Chez Ali" was in the Algerian qua...
...from the Bastille. Two or three days a week...
...with friends to sit drinking Algerian tea...
...y ~~Algerian~~ one of the staff would roll a huge cone shaped...
...I'd would smoke and drink tea ~~till~~ until...
...four when all the musicians came in. The...
...tes, hand drums of all kinds, guitars, man...
...couple of guys could really sing. Stan...
...llan Eager came through and as usual...
...about 45 minutes ... walking st...

In '56, Liliane's visa expired and she returned to Paris. I asked ABC to arrange for me to go to Europe for a while so I could be with her, and they did. During our last engagement in Chicago before the quartet broke up, Russ started having terrible migraine headaches. These headaches were so painful and lasted for such a long time that Russ had to quit and return to L.A. I decided to hire another rhythm section. I felt very good about the guys who joined the band. One of them, Dick Twadzick, had recently been discharged from the federal hospital in Lexington. He had been recommended to me by Peter Littman, a young drummer also from Boston. Dick and Peter had known each other for quite a while. Dick had studied with Serge Chaloff's mother, an excellent pianist and teacher. Another new member, Jimmy Bond, had recently graduated from Juilliard, where he had majored in string bass and tuba.

I flew to Paris a week ahead of the band, then drove down to meet their boat when they arrived. I was excited about the group. I think now that Dick started getting high from that first night, but I was not to find out about this fact for some months. At that point I was very naive about being strung out on stuff, although Liliane had also shown some interest in stuff; she had merely chipped around, never getting really strung out. Paris was full of people using in '56.

We appeared in concert at the Sal Playel in Paris. Dick's playing was always impeccable, as was Jimmy Bond's. If I had only been a little hipper, I might have been able to prevent what was soon to happen. We had just finished a concert somewhere in Switzerland and I was standing backstage speaking with people when there was a loud bang. Moving quickly toward the noise, as did everyone else, I saw Dick lying on the floor. He had passed out cold, and several people were trying to figure out what was wrong with him. We located a doctor and cleared the stage area. I should point out that Dick had always taken care of business; always at work on time and always playing exceptionally. He was a brilliant guy, really well-read. He had begun to speak French after only about a month in France. He was truly a gifted man, as were Peter and Jimmy. We revived Dick after his fall and continued to play gigs.

We returned to Paris to record a couple of albums for Nicole Barclay's Company and Blue Star Records. Bob Zieff and Dick Twadzick had been acquainted in Boston for some time. They were friends. Zieff had given Dick six or seven of his compositions, with arrangements for them, to bring to Europe. We recorded those compositions, and one of Dick's, all in one afternoon. They were beautiful. Zieff had titled some of them "Rondette," "Piece Caprice," "Sad Walk," "Mid Fort E," and "Pomp." Dick's was called "The Girl from Greenland": It seemed that he cared a lot for an Eskimo girl from Greenland, for I noticed he wrote to her often.

I found Bob Zieff's music a delight. Every line and harmony was different from the next, never going the way you thought it would, but somehow complete, logical, and unique. The day after recording Zieff's tunes, we were to record another album. Everyone showed up but Dick. We waited an hour, then Peter volunteered to go to his hotel room and see what was happening. About an hour later Peter rushed into the studio completely hysterical, screaming that Dick was dead. He said that he and the hotel manager had broken the door open and found Dick bright blue, the spike still in his arm. Dick's death brought things pretty much to an end for a while. I sent Jimmy back to the States and Peter and I hung around Paris a month or so. I recorded an album with the French musicians Pierre Michelot and Daniel Humair, met Barney Wilen, and worked with George Arvanitas, Bobby Jaspar, Jacques Pelzer, and Benoît Quersin, who were Belgian, and the Frenchman René Urtreger. I worked for the government in Germany, France, England, and Ireland—I was trying to keep busy.

I fired Peter during a concert at an Army base outside of Paris. He was acting too strange. Liliane and I split up and I returned to the States. I did several albums for Riverside for Bill Glover, usually with Kenny Drew, Paul Chambers, Bill Evans, and Johnny Griffin. I rehired Peter and hired Phil Urso on tenor and Bobby Timmons on piano, with Jimmy Bond on bass. We continued to play the old circuit of jazz clubs across the U.S. While appearing in Detroit at the Rouge Lounge, I met a woman named Halema. We were married about six months later. I began to get high more and more often, until finally I was hooked.

During the summer of '57, I was working at the Peacock Lane on the corner of Hollywood Boulevard and Western. I'd been ten to fifteen minutes late a couple of times and the manager of the club told me the next time I was late, I was fired. The following night I arrived about ten minutes late. As I crossed Hollywood, to my left, I saw two cops studying the outstretched arms of two friends of mine alongside the club under the streetlight, looking for marks. I parked about fifty feet up Western. Halema stayed in the car and I slipped into the club. The manager was standing in the aisle, between myself and the bandstand—there were no other people there yet. As I walked toward him I said, "I guess this means I'm fired?" He said only "Yes." I kept walking, picked up my trumpet, and stepped quickly back to the club entrance, out and across the street to my car.

The cops had been so intent on their game that they hadn't noticed me. I started the engine and shifted to low gear; as I did, an unmarked black Ford started to make a turn onto Western. I told Halema to hold on (she was seven months pregnant), and I hit the next corner in seconds, about a hundred yards ahead of one of the cops. I quickly made a left, then another left, and made my way to the freeway. I didn't see any more of them after the second left. I knew they wanted to bust me, but at that moment I had no idea just how preoccupied those two cops were with me. Believing that it might not be a good idea to return to my house for a while, I stopped and let Halema out before I reached the freeway entrance. I gave her some money, telling her to take a cab and that I would call her as soon as I had a chance.

I drove on to Balboa, arriving just an hour before a friend named Bobby Gill was leaving on his abalone boat for San Miguel Island for a week. I decided to cool it for a while, to clean up and let the sun work on my arms. I went with him. After the fourth day I began to feel a little better. During the day there were things to keep you occupied, to take your mind off how miserable you felt—things like the comforting warmth of the sun—but at night, with a thirty-degree drop in the temperature, everyone asleep, and no sound except the wind and the ocean slapping the hull, you had plenty of time to feel everything that was going on with your body. I finally slept a couple of hours on the sixth night.

Bobby Gill was a string guy. He'd run around on the bottom at one hundred feet down in his dry suit plucking abalone and stuffing them in his net sack. He'd then attach the full bag of abalone to the electric lag line, pull the line twice, and go back to work as the bag was pulled up, dumped, and dropped again. He'd stay down for about an hour, and during that time he'd gather ten to twelve dozen prime-size pinks. On the afternoon of the seventh day Bob suggested that I should go down and try it. I'd done a lot of diving, both skin- and Aqua-Lung, but I'd never been down with a helmet and air line. He put me in a suit, wrapping the back tightly with strips of inner tube, carefully tying it. I dropped off the boat ladder and held on to the bag line, sinking slowly to the bottom. The heavy lead shoes were a drag and took a bit of getting used to. I'd only been down a few minutes when I noticed that my feet were cold, much colder than they should have been. I started walking around. The seaweed was thick. It rose from the bottom like a great waving forest. I looked up at my air hose disappearing up into the seaweed. The cold had moved up to my waist. I walked in the direction of where my air hose disappeared, expecting to find the bag line. After five minutes of searching for the bag line, I realized that my air hose had doubled back—I had been walking in the wrong direction. By the time I found the bag line, the water had risen to my chest inside my leaking suit. I pulled twice on the line and was slowly pulled up. I grabbed for the ladder, missed, and began to sink back toward the bottom. Bob, realizing what had happened, quickly dropped the bag line; as the lead sinker went by me, I reached out and grabbed the line. The water was up to my neck as he unscrewed the helmet and calmly explained that the water wouldn't have come up into the mask because of the air pressure. The suit had been leaking in the back since I'd been in the water.

The next night I returned home, to learn exactly what happened to my two friends outside the club. One was only seventeen years old. The cops had taken him aside and made him an offer to drop the charges against him if he would sign a statement saying that I was the one who supplied him with the stuff. They told him he would go to jail for a long time if he didn't cooperate. He did, so now I had to get out of California. They must have been really mad about me getting away that night.

ten

ransferred to another prison to await tria
days of "Pentonville" I went to court. I ac
I take the whole thing too seriously. All t
ly pompous fools with their white wigs. I
, I was found guilty by his Lordship
believe the pharmacist's testimony that
't ask him to steal the drugs and I had
him anything for it. His Lordship se
I believe that I hadn't paid him to
ify. Back in "Pentonville" once again fo
s then to another prison where all the a
held and four days later I was accompanie
ry and deported to France. Carol and Jean, a
were
ry; She had arranged it with the po
[illegible] We'd been back in Pa
all
p when we were picked up by the police a
part of a 3 month investigation which c
arrest of about 150 people. We were all
suspected drug addiction. After about 5
began to cop out. As soon as somebod
their statement admitting guilt, they
into another room and given a fix of
s better than they could get on the street.

I headed east, getting as far as Las Vegas before I burned a valve. I laid low for a few days at Jimmy McKean's pad, then called the booking office and explained the situation to Joe Glazer. He arranged for a plane ticket for me, and I was soon back to work. My son Chetie was born a couple of months later in San Francisco. No one bothered me during this time. The next couple of years were difficult, however, with a continuous change of personnel in the band. I recorded another album of Bob Zieff songs with cello, string bass, bass clarinet, French horn, oboe, and flügelhorn. The album was never released, though, because the record company decided that it just wasn't commercial enough.

I got busted again while driving back from Chicago to Milwaukee after having copped some stuff. A black cat and some black chicks were in the car with me. The guy had just gotten out of jail after serving five years. I cut them loose and spent a terrible four days in the Waukegan jail before Halema got me out on bail.

Returning to New York, I got busted in Harlem. Again, I was bailed out. I decided to check into Lexington Federal Hospital. After three days of methadone, they put me in skid row (isolation for addicts), watched me a couple of days, then put me in population. I was surprised to find so many guys, particularly musicians, that I knew.

Tadd Dameron was in charge of the band, whose members did nothing all day every day but set up on the big stage in the auditorium and rehearse. I wrote the judge in Waukegan a letter explaining what I'd done, and he subsequently dropped the charges.

I managed to get into a private room after a couple of nights of sleeping in the hospital hall. Mike, an old friend and connection from San Francisco, had gotten busted on his bike while running some stuff somewhere. He'd managed to get away from them a couple of times, but those federal men are not dumb. He'd been at Lexington for two or three years. His job there was to run the projector on Sundays for the weekly movie, and rumor had it that he was one of the few men able to get into the women's section. I didn't sleep for seventeen days and nights—it was like the boat all over again.

After I'd been at Kentucky about ten days, I received a kite through Mike from a girl I'd met in Detroit; she used to come in the Rouge Lounge almost every night. She said she'd see me at the rehearsal for the Christmas show. I was surprised to see how much weight she'd lost—she really looked good. She must have been making it with one of the black guys, judging from the looks I was getting from them. We were able to sit next to one another during the rehearsal. She told me she had checked into

Kentucky only because she'd heard that I was there. We arranged to check out on the same day, a couple of weeks from then. We met in town and took the train to New York. I spent a couple of weeks at her apartment, but unfortunately some joker ripped off the door of her Corvette when I was using the car. He didn't even stop. We had a few words about that, and fought about some other things as well. It all ended in my telling her to get fucked.

I hung around New York, running around up in Harlem every day. A guy named Dirty Nick lived on 143d near Lenox Avenue. He'd been dealing for a well-known supplier but there had been some trouble and he'd been replaced. He'd probably come to the man short of money once too often. For several days I'd been coming to his pad and I'd wait while he went out to cop. He'd come back and we'd get off. I'd usually be tired and nod off, only to wake up with cockroaches crawling all over me.

This particular day, neither of us had any money. Nick suggested running a game on his old boss. He explained everything as we waited in my little black Ford on Seventh Avenue between 125th and 126th Streets. We watched as a dark-blue Cadillac pulled up next to a bar on the corner of 126th, but across the street from us. We continued to watch as, one by one, each of the boss's runners stepped up to the side of the car and were told where their packages were to be found, at what addresses. A big black dude—they were all black dudes—received his address and flagged a cab; we followed.

The cab headed uptown and stopped in front of a corner apartment house at 165th and Amsterdam. I let him get inside the front door, then followed him in. This guy weighed about two hundred pounds. As I came through the front door, he jumped to his feet. He'd been searching underneath the radiator, and when he saw me, he almost shit. I didn't give him any time to think. I weighed all of 140, but I was dressed in a blue suit, white shirt. No tie, but I was white, which is what I think upset him more than anything. "FBI," I said. "What are you doing in here?" While he stuttered, I kept talking. "Against the wall," I said. He turned around and I shook him down: no gun. He finally got out that he was there to visit a friend on the second floor. "Let's go see," I said. I followed him up the stairs. He knocked on the door. We waited. No one came. "No one at home," I said. "All right, man, beat it, and don't let me see you around here again." He was gone in a flash and I reached into the radiator and pulled out the stuff.

eleven

she
gives birth. The government gives
for every new-born child, for blankets
ge and other stuff a baby needs. They
de free milk for the first 6 mos. to
the child gets off to a good start. I
crazy around London and finally
into trouble with the law. Lady
write a script for friday, one for
for sunday because she always
country estate somewhere outside
weekends. As I cashed my
I noticed that there was a new
macist. He seemed very friendly and
lunch, Since I hadn't much money
ted. During lunch he said he like
wanted to help me out, I told him
need any help, ~~that~~ I got all the
eded on prescription. As I left I
appreciated his kindness but no thank
at midnight, when the predated scripts
something. The addicts were lined
their scripts filled and people were
up and down the line trying to get

In the spring of '59 my New York case came up, and I got six months on Rikers Island. I spent about ten days' time in the infirmary and was then put in population. I was assigned a job as an instructor in the music department. There were about a dozen other musicians there. We spent all day in the gym either rehearsing or playing basketball. In the cell block at night there were poker games, bridge, chess, reading, or watching a couple who were great dancers; I remember one was called "Baby Lawrence."

I got out after four months (good behavior) and left immediately for Europe. Halema and Chetie came with me. After the first festival of Comblain La Tour I went to Italy. I began using Jetrium, a German pharmaceutical product that you could get without a prescription. I'd fly from Milan to Munich with no baggage, and then fill the pockets of my heavy coat with boxes of injectable Jetrium (double strength, 13.5 mgs. per cc.), then fly back to Italy. Jetrium was the closest thing to stuff that I'd ever found, but I quickly built up a resistance to it since I was using 1,000 to 1,200 mgs. a day. I was in bad shape—chalky-colored, not eating, and having terrible, frequent chills. Friends convinced me to see a doctor. After his examination and analysis the doctor gave me four to six months to live if I continued my Jetrium habit. I gave notice where I'd been working—at a place called the Santa Tecla—and signed myself into the Villa Turo clinic in Milan for a sleep cure. I slept for seven days, being fed intravenously by huge bottles suspended above me. I felt no discomfort from withdrawal and thirty days later managed, with the help of the American consulate, to get out thirty days ahead of schedule.

I felt fine and returned to the Santa Tecla, where, while working one night, I met Carol. She was working at the Olympia, one of the largest clubs in the world (1,600 seats) as one of four girl announcers, each of whom announced a segment of the show. Sometimes I'd jump in my Alfa and race to the Olympia between sets, just to walk around backstage. It was crazy: There were so many costumed and scantily clad ladies running all over the place. It was great. I fell for Carol, and she left the show to travel with me. The Italian papers made a big thing of Carol and me. Halema sent Chetie to stay with my folks and followed me around for a while. We had some terrible scenes in a few clubs when she would show up. I began to go to a couple of different doctors each week, asking them to write me prescriptions. I had one good doctor just across the border in Switzerland, but I never took much. I kept my habit to a minimum.

While working at La Bussola, a beautiful, expensive

high-class club on the beach at Focette, about a mile from Viareggio, I met Dr. Lippi Francesconi. He was the medical director of a small clinic in Lucca. I moved into the clinic Santa Zita, receiving large daily doses of vitamins and other medications, plus a diminishing dose of Palfium. By this time I was getting very hard to hit—my veins were collapsing and disappearing. Dr. Francesconi drove me to work every night, waited while I played, and then drove me back to the clinic. Carol met me at the club each night. We had a room in a *pensione,* the Villa Gemma. The manager tried to help me, before I went back to the clinic, by having a doctor write a Palfium prescription in his name for me. Another good friend, an attorney visiting Italy, also had a script written in his name for me.

One day I had to go to the club during the day. Dr. Francesconi couldn't get away, so I rented a Fiat and started toward the beach. I stopped in a gas station to give myself an injection. It took me forty-five minutes to get a hit. I had just finished cleaning up and was ready to leave when there was a knock on the door. The station attendant had called the police. They said I would have to come with them to the station. Once there, they called Dr. Francesconi, who explained everything and drove over to pick me up. The next day the headline of the local paper read CHET BAKER FOUND IN GAS STATION TOILET. Continuing on, I read that the police had been forced to break down the door, that the toilet was covered in blood, etc., etc. A young prosecutor named Romiti, after reading the newspaper account, started an investigation. After checking all the pharmacies in the area and examining all Palfium scripts, he arrested my attorney friend Joey Carani, the guy who ran the *pensione,* a doctor named Bechelli, and Dr. Francesconi. He then traveled to Milan to question Halema. Having no jurisdiction in Milan, he lied to her, telling her that he wanted her to come back to Lucca for further questioning. She went, and upon her arrival he promptly arrested her, too.

Naturally, I was the first to be locked up. They put me in the infirmary for ten days, then moved me to a segregated room where I spent the next six months. No one spoke a word of English. At night I could hear Halema, across the courtyard, crying and crying. We all went to court after six months. At the trial, Halema, Joey, Francesconi, and the guy who ran the Gemma were all found not guilty. Only Bechelli and I remained locked up. Bechelli got two years because he had been charging me ten thousand lire for each of the scripts. I got eighteen months for illegal use. We appealed three months later, and he got cut loose and my sentence was reduced to fifteen months.

Carol remained in Italy until after the trial, along with her mother, then they both returned to England. She wrote me every day, and even on Sundays I received letters from her. The prison priest, Father Ricci, read all my incoming and outgoing mail. Carol would subsequently receive letters from me completely crossed out with black ink. I realized that this fool, rather than admit he couldn't read English, was just crossing out everything. He would also rip out all the pictures in the *Playboy* magazines Carol would send me.

After the trial I was allowed to work in the bookbinding shop, whose sole occupant was a Yugoslavian resistance fighter, a little guy who had been supporting himself since the end of the war by impersonating officers, entering military bases, and ripping them off for all kinds of arms and ammunition. He had been there forty-four months and had not yet been to court. We played chess all day while I watched him repair and re-cover books. In the evenings, he'd cook up a big pot of spaghetti sauce on an illegal hot plate, causing the lights to dim throughout the whole prison whenever he plugged it in.

At this point, I'd gotten pretty tight with a couple of guards. One guard in particular, named Peccora, would leave Carol and me alone in the visiting room. That was nice—I doubt if anyone can appreciate what a little sex can mean until they've been locked up in segregation for a few months. The guards finally found our hot plate, and my assigned job became delivering food and other things that were ordered by the inmates. Every week Carol would send me fifteen to twenty paperback books, and I would read and read at night by the light of my five-watt bulb. I had my horn and would play a couple of hours every day. I wrote thirty-two songs, and the time passed quickly.

By the time of my release I spoke fluent Italian, and while I'd been locked up I had gotten a visit from some film company in Rome. I signed a contract giving them the rights to a screenplay about me in which I would do the soundtrack. They gave me three thousand dollars in advance, and upon my release I would receive so much a week until the film was finished, up to twenty-five thousand dollars.

The same paper that was responsible for starting the whole mess made a big thing out of my release. Photographers followed Carol and me around, taking hundreds of pictures. Many of these found their way into several of the Italian scandal magazines, along with a completely made-up story. RCA Italiana sent one of their representatives to see me in Milan, and I signed a contract to record some of the tunes I had composed for which lyrics were being written.

Carol and I drove to Rome in a new Alfa SS and checked into a small exclusive hotel in Parioli. We hung around for a couple of weeks after the record date, just to see what was going to happen with the film. Nothing went down, so I went back to work in Italy. I hired René Thomas and Bobby Jaspar for my band. They were both great players but screwed up with drugs. Bobby was using Ritalin and René was in constant search of stuff. We played at a club in Napoli and some bastard ripped off my horn during a break. I figured it was because they used to call me "Trombo Doro," and whoever took it must've thought that it was solid gold.

The next seven months were good ones for me. Oriana Fallaci did a big article about me in *L'Europea* and I appeared in an Italian film called *Ulatori alla sbarra.* I portrayed a constantly nodding-out dude who occasionally wakes up and sings a song—when he's not putting around Rome on a Vespa.

Nineteen sixty-one was the year of the beginning of the electric music scene in Rome, and many restaurants had poets reciting a new kind of poetry, occasionally accompanied by a flute or hand drum. I could never get into it too much. I did several soundtracks for some documentary films produced by the Italian government, some with snare drum and trumpet, some with trumpet only. I would just watch the film and play whatever came into my head. After I returned to Milan, it was arranged through Nando Latanzzi that I do a night of jazz at the Olympia, which was a huge success.

During a conversation with Nando that night, I mentioned that I'd like to have my own club. He took me to a small, very elegant room that was not in use. It had a small service bar, a raised bandstand with beautiful velvet drapes, colored lights, marble-top tables, and plush blue-velvet armchairs with matching carpet throughout. We began rehearsing there every night. Nando ordered and installed a neon sign that read THE CHET BAKER CLUB. Each night after rehearsal, Nando would lay out a spaghetti dinner for us all: the waiters, bartenders, musicians, everyone. We'd push four of five tables together, eat, and then, after the dishes were removed, play poker or blackjack. I'd go back to the Hotel Virgilio with my pockets stuffed with those big old ten-thousand-lire notes.

A week before the grand opening of the club, during a rehearsal, I had an unexpected visit from three black cats. They had just come from Beirut. They were practically in tears when I told them that I was clean and not into anything, and that I couldn't help them score. They left, but the next night they came back again, this time with even more desperate pleas for me to help them out. I drove with them to Chiasso and told them where to go and what to say. Within minutes one of them, Donald Brown, came back with a bottle of Palfium tablets. All in all, a successful outing.

At this time, my own musicians were all Italian. They were the best players in Italy at that time: Amadeo Tommasi on piano, Giovanni Tommasso on bass, and Franco Mondini on drums. Amadeo was still attending a music conservatory in Bologna. He liked Paul Chambers and Ray Brown. He and his brother, a pianist, had a group called La Cinque di Lucci. They were from just outside Firenze. Franco, whose father was a doctor, was from Torino.

At the time I was working at the Bussola in Viareggio, I'd been appearing with Romano Mussolini, who seemed very nice but very shy. Everything he played sounded like the blues. He could play "Stardust" and make it come out somehow sounding like the blues. Hampton Hawes had this same quality, but Romano lacked the fire and imagination of Hawes.

A few days before the opening of my club I traveled to Munich to play a concert and got in some trouble. I wasn't prosecuted, but they did hold me for three weeks. I was finally released, and a German police-officer driver drove Carol and me and Donald Brown (who was with us) back to the Swiss border. We crossed Switzerland and, upon attempting to enter Italy, I was refused entrance. I sent Carol on to Milan, since she was okay with the authorities, and she managed to borrow 150,000 lire from Mario Fatori, an acquaintance of ours who owned a big studio where he made commercials for movie houses and TV.

After Carol returned from Milan with the money, we left for Paris. I really hated leaving the club—and my Alfa—behind, and Carol and I both had to leave behind a lot of clothes and stuff. Within a week of our arrival in Paris, I began to work with Bud Powell and Kenny Clarke at the Blue Note. The club was managed by a nice guy named Ben Benjamin. It was one of those fairly common situations where a wife owns the club but her husband manages it. I really disliked Ben's wife, so much that I was relieved when I was contacted about going to England to do a bit in a movie starring Susan Hayward.

twelve

y breathe. The kitchen was the only room that
Each day in the Jackson home began with
other, getting up first, dressing in the cold,
the kitchen to light the oven and heat water
[illegible]. 20 minutes later she would c
l to get moving, that he would be late for
and him a large mug of tea as he came in.
a stool near the oven, a tiny white poodle a
gging and whining for some tea. "Want your tea
y to the dog as it danced around his feet,
d down and fill the saucer; over and over.
d split the mug. Al was an inventor wh
late into the night in his work shop shed o
k. He had designed and built a new ty
which would either double the miles p
the distance on the same amount of f
ied to get something going with seve
ted Co's but they always wanted 5
wanted to keep control. He was an
without a degree; forced to do odd
ntry or electrical work in order to get b
ve birth on Christmas morning. The sur
him sed; he was the first child born

Our first day in England, Donald Brown and I went to 32 Wimpole Street to see Lady Isabella MacDougal Frankau. She was about seventy-five years old, white-haired, and very businesslike. She didn't ask me for much information about myself. She had already heard of my antics all over Europe. She simply asked my name, my address, and how much cocaine and heroin I wanted per day. I started with ten grams of each, having had little experience with buying cocaine or heroin at the corner drugstore. Ten grams of heroin in 1/6 gram tablets turned out to be sixty tablets that were the same size as standard diluted tabs. The coke was about what you would get for five hundred dollars in New York, but pure. The whole script cost only about three and a half dollars. After that first day my scripts were all for twenty grams of each, and I was off and running under that old English drug system.

Lady Frankau seemed to like me, possibly because I was working at least, whereas most of her 250 to 300 patients were unemployed and unable to do much more than hustle a few pills here and there to pay the rent and eat. For the next nine months I stayed with Carol at her folks' home. Her father was a little Cockney guy who had never seen a dope fiend in his life. I gave him a fit. When Carol had quit her job in Italy and began traveling around with me, all kinds of stories about me and our relationship reached her mother and father. One story said that I had abducted Carol and was keeping her with me against her will by giving her heroin. That story actually came out in a scandal paper in London. Naturally, when Carol's father started getting phone calls about us and reading all the bullshit in the papers, he decided to find out for himself. He and Carol's mother arrived in Rome one evening while I was appearing at an exclusive supper club on the Via Veneto, called the Rupe Tarpea. One look at Carol and they knew everything was cool; she was dressed in a dark-green sequined evening dress and she looked beautiful. Her father explained to us about all the publicity and crap in the papers. One newspaper even printed a story claiming Interpol was looking for us.

They remained in Rome a couple of days and returned to England, satisfied that their daughter was not being abused by some maniac, but the situation was different now that I was living with them. I was using again, and Carol was pregnant. Under the circumstances, I'd have to give them both an A for remaining calm and cool (well, most of the time). Carol and I found out later that most of the stories had been supplied to the press and to her parents by the other three girls she had worked with at the Olympia.

I began to work immediately on the film, which was

being done at the Shepperton Studios. Since I had to be there so early in the morning and had to stay there all day, it was impossible to see Lady Frankau. I'd have to call her around nine-thirty in the morning, and she'd then write the prescription and have it delivered to the pharmacy near her office. The pharmacist would make up my package, call a taxi, and have it brought to me at Shepperton. I would disappear into my trailer on the lot and fix speedballs until someone called for me.

When the picture was finished—along with my work permit—Lady Frankau arranged, with her influence, for me to stay on in England. She lied for me, claiming I was too sick to travel. I think I was only able to give her money for about the first three or four months. After that, I hadn't any money left, and she allowed me to fill my scripts at the pharmacy on her account. I couldn't work, because you had to live in England for one year to be able to join the musicians' union, so I spent most of my days and nights just hanging out and getting high with other people just as screwed up as I was.

One guy I met during this time drove a minicab and offered to run me home one day. During the trip he managed to cook up, draw up, and give himself a fix right through his hip pants leg, all while ripping through the evening traffic. Of course, when we got to the house he asked if he could come in and fix. I let him in and we had fixed a couple of times when he started hallucinating, saying somebody was on the roof trying to take his picture. The next thing I knew, he unlocked the screen and jumped out on the roof. He was there when Carol's father came home. I heard Al yelling, "What the hell are you doing up there?" at this fool. He jumped down and ran, in a complete panic, for his car. I never saw him again.

The winter of 1962–63 in England was the coldest in one hundred years. If it weren't for Carol's body heat in bed, I think I would have frozen to death. I'd wake up every morning with a frost on my upper lip from my breath. The kitchen was the only room that was warm. Each day in the Jackson home began with Gladys, Carol's mother, getting up first, dressing in the cold, then slipping down to the kitchen to light the oven and heat the water for tea. Twenty minutes later she would call up to Al to get moving, yelling that he would be late for work. She'd hand him a large mug of tea as he came into the kitchen and sat on a stool near the oven, with their tiny white poodle at his feet, begging and whining for some tea. "Want your tea, do ya," he'd say, pouring a bit into the dog's saucer. This was repeated over and over until they had split the mug.

Al was an inventor who worked late into the night in

his workshop shed out in the back. He had designed and built a new type of propeller that would either double the user's speed or double the distance on the same amount of fuel. He'd tried to get something going with several interested companies, but they always wanted to own 51 percent of the patent, and he wanted to keep control. He was an engineer without a degree, and therefore forced to do odd jobs, carpentry, and electrical work in order to get by.

Carol gave birth on Christmas morning. The nurses named him Red—he was the first child born that morning. The official Christmas baby. He was a perfect baby, seven pounds, seven ounces, with blue eyes and reddish-brown hair. I went with Al to visit Carol. We walked about two miles over the iced-over road to reach the hospital. The last quarter-mile we had to wade through two feet of snow to reach the main buildings. Carol and the baby were fine. In England a woman must remain in the hospital for ten days when she gives birth. The government gives a certain amount of money for every newborn child, for the purchase of blankets, a carriage, and all the other stuff a baby needs. They also provide free milk for the first six months to make sure the child gets off to a good start.

I continued to act crazy around London, and finally

managed to get into trouble with the law. Lady Frankau would typically write a script for Friday, one for Saturday, and one for Sunday because she always went to her country estate somewhere outside of London for the weekends. As I cashed my Friday script I noticed that there was a new young pharmacist. He seemed very friendly and invited me to lunch. Since I hadn't much money I accepted. During lunch he said he liked me and wanted to help me out. I told him I didn't need any help, that I got all the stuff I needed on the prescription. As I left I told him I appreciated his kindness, but no thanks.

Friday at midnight, when the predated scripts became good, it was really something. The addicts were lined up having their scripts filled, and people were running up and down the line, trying to get a gram here and a gram there. Some people were so sick, or believed that they were, that they would stop in the alleyways right on the street and cook up and fix right there, with square customers walking around them. The closest, safest place to fix was the public toilet about a half a block's walk from the drugstore. Between midnight and one o'clock you could smell the strong odor of sulphur in the toilet as people cooked up in the semiprivacy of their stalls.

Monday morning the sweet pharmacist smiled as I handed him my script, saying, "Meet me at the bookstore around the corner at ten o'clock. I have a present for you." Fool that I was, I went. At ten he walked in and handed me a cigarette box, said, "This is for you," and left. I stepped out into the street and opened the box. It contained a full vial of coke that barely fit in the box. This guy has got to be crazy, I thought. I knew that the pharmacist in charge kept a tally by weight, and that they would find out before very long that there were one hundred grams missing. I walked a block to the room of a guy and his old lady that I knew, and by four o'clock we had used up all the coke.

The police came four days later. All of a sudden, as they walked into the house, I thought, I've been set up. They had no evidence—none of the coke or its container was there. The only thing they had was the pharmacist's statement that he had given it to me, but they arrested me anyway and delivered me to the station house, where I was told I would have to spend the whole weekend awaiting my court appearance Monday morning. I explained to the sergeant that I was an addict, and that my doctor was Dr. Frankau. He called her and verified my story, and within two hours a large manila envelope arrived at the jail. Every four hours, one of the guards would bring me the envelope and I'd fix in my cell. On Monday morning Carol and Al were in the courtroom, and I was released into Al's custody. After that, Al and I had many discussions about my getting straight again. I had Lady Frankau arrange for me to go into a private clinic, but I remained there only a few days.

I came down with blood poisoning quite suddenly one day while I was out screwing around. I flagged a cab and told him to take me to the nearest hospital. The nurse in emergency asked me what was happening. I told her that my head was splitting and that I'd been throwing up. She took my temperature, and it was 104. They admitted me and started shooting me full of penicillin, and every four hours the nurse brought me a syringe, placed the partitions around my bed, and I'd fix. After four days, I left the hospital against the advice of the doctor.

A week later, Al withdrew his responsibility on my bail, and I was taken into custody and placed in population as if I were clean and in good shape. After lying in my cell for about twenty-four hours I started yelling and banging on my cell door with my shoe. A half hour later I was carried to the infirmary by four guards and dumped, naked, into a padded cell. I couldn't believe it. I didn't mind being in the padded cell or being naked, but it was so cold in there. Maybe that was part of their psychology, to keep you so worried about freezing that you wouldn't have a chance to think about how sick you were.

The next day, a doctor had the door opened, looked at me for five seconds from where he was, and without saying a word disappeared, the door banging shut again. An hour later the door opened and I was transferred to another prison to await trial. After fifteen days at Pentonville I went to court. I really couldn't take the whole thing too seriously. All those seemingly pompous fools with their white wigs. Needless to say, I was found guilty by his lordship, who didn't believe the pharmacist's testimony explaining that I had neither asked him to steal the coke nor paid him anything for it. His lordship simply did not believe that I hadn't paid him to steal the stuff. I was back in Pentonville once again, this time for another fifteen days, and then on to another prison where all the aliens were held. Four days later I was accompanied to the ferry and deported to France. Carol and Dean, our son, were on the ferry. Carol had arranged it beforehand with the police.

thirteen

e friend in his life. I gave him a fit.
~~had~~ quit her job in ITALY and began travel
with me, all kinds of stories about me and
ched her father and mother. One story ~~was~~ ~~circu~~
I ~~was~~ had abducted Carol, and was keeping her
ainst her will by giving her heroin. That sto
ly came out in a scandal paper in London. Natu
Carols father started getting phone calls about
ading all the bullshit in the papers, he decide
it for himself. He and Carols mother arrived
ne evening while I was appearing at an exclu
club on the via Veneto, the Rupe Tarpea. One l
Carol and they knew everything was cool, she wa
in a dark green sequined evening dress and
autiful. He explained about all the publicity
the papers. One newspaper even print ~~the~~ a sto
looking for us. They remained in Roma a coup
nd returned to England, satisfied that their dau
t being abused by some maniac, but this w
t now. I was using again and Carol knew
t. Under the circumstances, I'd have to giv
it. A for remaining cool and calm; most of th
d I found out later that most of the stories ab

We'd been back in Paris only three or four days when we were all picked up by the police again. It was part of a three-month-long investigation that culminated in the arrest of over 150 people. We were all being held for suspicion of drug addiction. After about five or six hours of questioning, people began to cop out. As soon as somebody signed their statement admitting guilt, they were taken into another room and given a fix of stuff that was better than any they could get on the street. Poor baby Dean was only two months old and getting really hungry. After eight hours I was finally able to communicate with one of the detectives enough to convince him that I was not sick and that I had only been in France for a few days. By the time they let us go, over one hundred people had copped out and had been locked up, many of whom I knew.

I began working at a little *cave* in the Rue de la Huchette, called Le Chat Qui Pêche. An elderly woman named Madame Ricard owned the club. She lived in an apartment upstairs. The police continued to hassle me for a long time. Every month I'd receive a telegram from some inspector and within twenty-four hours I'd have to present myself to his office for an examination if I wanted to continue to remain in France. Business was good at the club. Carol would bring Dean down to the *cave* every night to be passed up and down the bar, since everyone wanted to hold him.

I worked with many European musicians during the next eleven months. I saw Anita O'Day and John Poole when they flew in from Denmark to cop some hash. The Chez Ali was in the Algerian quarter not far from the Bastille. Two or three days a week I'd go there with friends to sit drinking Algerian tea while watching one of the staff roll a huge cone-shaped cigarette. We would smoke and drink tea until around four, when all the musicians came in. They had flutes, hand drums of all kinds, guitars, and mandolins. A couple of guys could really sing, too. Stan Getz and Allen Eager came through, and as usual I spent forty-five minutes walking Stan around the fourth floor of a hotel hallway to keep him from nodding out, with Allen on one side of him and me on the other. Dexter came through and hung out for a while as well. I sent a couple of people to England to see Lady Frankau. They all came back with heroin and coke.

Nineteen sixty-three was a very good year. I managed to keep from getting strung out too badly. I stayed clean for four or five months, much to the amazement of the French authorities, who demanded a monthly urine specimen. When they finally let me off the hook, I began to get high once in a while, usually upon the return of someone I'd referred to Lady Frankau in London. They would always come back with a nice taste of heroin and cocaine. Sometimes I would cop from the ex-wife of an old friend, but the stuff wasn't much good—it had been stepped on so many times, you had to shoot a half a spoon to feel anything, and then the high was gone in twenty minutes.

Madame Ricard's Chat Qui Pêche *cave* was packed every night. Musicians from all over Europe came in to play and have a bowl of Madame Ricard's homemade chili. My horn was stolen out of the kitchen there, and a French trumpet player lent me his flügelhorn, an old French Selmer. I loved the sound of it. He eventually gave it to me and I kept it for five years, using it on all the albums I recorded in 1964–65. I even used it for *Colpix,* the best jazz album of '64–65, which featured Phil Urso, Hal Galper, Charlie Rice, Jymie Merritt, Bobby Scott, and Kenny Burrell, and on *Limelight* with Baby Breeze. Eventually, most of us returned to the States, including myself.

I remember thinking about something that went down in '56 that I call "the Baltimore Affair." I had played in Baltimore many times in the past, usually at the old Comedy

Club, which is no longer around. I always stayed at the same little motel, ten or twelve miles from the city. A friend of mine named Bryce Wilson was traveling with the band, helping out with the packing, unpacking, driving, etc. I was sharing a room with another musician who was geeting high fairly often and messing with a lot of sleepers. He smoked all the time, was chipping, and taking Tuinal and Seconal. Despite all this, he was a wonderful musician, but people taking sleepers would do some strange things.

This particular night we'd had a couple of friends follow us back to the motel. This guy Abe was with us, whom I'd met the first time I came to Baltimore. He was short and heavy, loved playing the horses and smoking good grass—he always had some on him. This time, he'd also brought along a small homemade water pipe that quickly zonked us all, forcing me to crash at around four o'clock that morning. Bryce fell asleep soon after. At around six, voices from the dim distance pulled me back. The other guy staying with us was explaining to Bryce that he'd had an accident, that he'd hit the back of someone else's car, but that everything was okay. The police had driven him back to the motel because he'd forgotten to take his license. He grabbed the wallet and went out. It was a really close call, with the cops waiting right outside. Bryce and I looked at one another after he left and just shook our heads. One of us should have gone with him, but we were so stoned and so sleepy that we just couldn't.

postscript

Barcelona was beautiful in December of '63. After Paris, it seemed almost tropical. I made a deal to work a month in a cellar club that had been presenting jazz players for a year or so. Upstairs, Antonio Gades was dancing to the accompaniment of guitars, claves, and castanets. The club also furnished a small apartment in the deal. I began to make doctors write me scripts of Palfium. During the engagement I met a very prominent and well-connected family and, through them, a doctor with his own new and ultramodern clinics and operating room. He was a surgeon whose skill and facilities brought patients from all over the world. I was soon obtaining scripts from him, and it all began once again.

selected discography

10/53	**chet baker quartet**	Pacific Jazz PJLP-3 (10″)
10/53	**chet baker quartet featuring russ freeman**	Pacific Jazz PJLP-6 (10″)
12/53	**chet baker ensemble**	Pacific Jazz PJLP-9 (10″)
12/53 -2/54	**chet baker and strings**	Columbia CL-549
2/54	**chet baker sings**	Pacific Jazz PJLP-11 (10″)
5/54	**jazz at ann arbor**	World Pacific WP-1203
9/54	**chet baker sextet**	Pacific Jazz PJLP-15 (10″)
10/55	**rondette**	Barclay BLP-84009 (France)
10/55	**summertime**	Barclay BLP-84017 (France)
11/55	**alone together**	Barclay BLP-84042 (France)
7/56	**chet baker and crew**	World Pacific WP-1224
12/57	**reunion (w/jerry mulligan)**	Pacific Jazz Stereo 47
2/58	**stan meets chet (w/stan getz)**	Verve MGV-8263
8/58	**it could happen to you**	Riverside RLP12-278

9/58	**in new york**	Riverside RLP12-281
3/59	**ballads by chet baker**	Riverside RLP12-299
9/59	**chet baker in milan**	Vogue LD-526 (France) Jazzland JLP-918S (Italy)
1/62	**chet is back**	RCA LPM-10307 (Italy) RCA RGP-1182-M (Japan)
2/65	**baby breeze**	Limelight LS-86003
4/65	**cool burnin'**	Prestige PR-7495
10/66	**into my life (w/ the carmel strings)**	World Pacific WP-1858
4/70	**blood, chet, and tears**	Verve VG-8798
2/77	**you can't go home again**	A&M Horizon SP-726
8/78	**two a day**	All Life AL-007 (France)
1/79	**broken wing**	Sonopresse SP-251 (France)